KU-620-726

# CONTENTS

vi    Foreword

1    Introduction

3    1. New aims for a new
National Curriculum,
*John White*

41    2. A curriculum for the nation,
*Richard Aldrich*

64    References

## FOREWORD

Perspectives on Education Policy is a new series of publications from the Institute of Education, University of London, which focuses upon developments in education policy. It is anticipated that contributions to the series will be made across the Institute's academic groups and disciplines and that it will present and review research and evidence related to policy developments.

The first in the series, from the Institute's History and Philosophy academic group, reflects upon the curriculum of schools at a time when a major review of the curriculum is being undertaken for the year 2000. The paper is also 'first' in another sense, being the first from the Broader Perspectives Unit which has been established in the History and Philosophy academic group.

It is hoped that this new series will provide a helpful perspective on debate and discussion attending policy proposals and formulation.

**PROFESSOR PETER MORTIMORE**
Director, Institute of Education

February 1998

# THE NATIONAL CURRICULUM BEYOND 2000: THE QCA AND THE AIMS OF EDUCATION

Liverpool John Moores University
LEARNING & INFO SERVICES

Accession
Number DA                    K

Class
Number

Site          A

**Institute of Education**
UNIVERSITY OF LONDON

# The National Curriculum beyond 2000: the QCA and the aims of education

**Richard Aldrich**
PROFESSOR OF THE
HISTORY OF EDUCATION

**John White**
PROFESSOR OF
PHILOSOPHY OF EDUCATION

LIVERPOOL JMU LIBRARY

3 1111 00974 3327

First published in 1998 by the
Institute of Education University of London,
20 Bedford Way, London WC1H 0AL
Tel: 0171-580 1122. Fax: 0171-612 6126

*Pursuing Excellence in Education*

© Institute of Education University of London 1998

British Library Cataloguing in Publication Data:
a catalogue record for this publication is available
from the British Library

ISBN 0 85473 553 4

Produced in Great Britain by
Reprographic Services
Institute of Education University of London

Printed by Formara Limited
16 The Candlemakers, Temple Farm Industrial
Estate, Southend on Sea, Essex SS2 5RX

I1/0001-PEP No.1-0298

# Introduction

The National Curriculum was introduced in 1988. Although in the last ten years its content has been modified in detail, it has only very recently been subjected to fundamental review. This has been carried out over the past year by the Qualifications and Curriculum Authority, whose report is due to go to the Secretary of State for Education and Employment in Spring 1998.

A key feature of QCA's review has been the attention it has paid to the purposes of education. Its early discussions with teachers, teaching organizations, local authorities and researchers revealed 'that many believe that the present statutory arrangements, including the National Curriculum, lack a clear vision of what the parts, individually and collectively, are designed to achieve'. This reinforced the QCA's view that there needs to be 'a much clearer statement about the aims and priorities of the school curriculum as a necessary preliminary to any review' (QCA, 1997).

It is not surprising that so many bodies have been calling for a more adequate account of aims. The aims of the maintained school curriculum stated in the 1988 Educational Reform Act were both excessively brief and thin on substance. They were: to promote 'the spiritual, moral, cultural, mental and physical development of pupils at the school and of society'; and to 'prepare such pupils for the opportunities, responsibilities and experiences of adult life'. A curriculum for a nation deserves better than this. QCA has been conducting a wide-ranging consultation seeking general agreement on the aims of the school curriculum. This has included questionnaires sent to every maintained school asking for their views on this issue at the different key stages. The results will be fed into the report sent to David Blunkett this Spring. As far as is known, the QCA exercise is the first in-depth investigation by any official body in Britain of what the aims of school education should be.

The two papers included in this publication spring from the QCA initiative on aims and have been fed into the consultation process. 'New aims for a new National Curriculum' by John White, Professor of Philosophy of Education at the Institute of Education, asks the methodological question: how should one go about determining what curricular aims should be? It looks at problems with various answers, including the appeal to consensus that QCA is adopting. Positively, it suggests that the only clear way of identifying aims which avoids privileging the preferences of a section of the population is to derive them from values implicit in the notion of democracy itself.

Richard Aldrich is Professor of the History of Education at the Institute of Education. His 'A Curriculum for the Nation' focuses on two questions. The first is: what are the main strengths and weaknesses of common curricula in general and of the National Curriculum in particular? The second, given that the aims and content of school curricula have been debated for centuries, is: what lessons may be drawn from an historical perspective upon these issues? In considering this latter question, particular emphasis is placed upon the writings of John Locke, the seventeenth century political and educational thinker.

The two essays in this volume are the first fruits of the Broader Perspectives Unit set up in late 1997 within the History and Philosophy Group at the Institute of Education. A central purpose of this unit is to bring historical and philosophical thinking to bear on issues of current importance in the field of educational policy. It will be producing further publications in this Institute of Education series in response to matters of urgent practical concern.

# 1
# New aims for a new National Curriculum

**JOHN WHITE**
Professor of Philosophy of Education
Institute of Education University of London

## ABSTRACT

*This paper originates from and engages with QCA's current drive to collect opinion from different constituencies about what the aims of a revised national curriculum should be after 2000. It asks the methodological question: how should one go about determining what curricular aims should be? Its critical section looks at various answers, including the appeal to consensus which QCA is adopting, none of which, however, avoids the problem of sectionalism. The positive section argues that aims should be rooted in the democratic constitution of our polity itself, showing in more detail what the substance of such aims should be and how such general aims might be realized in more determinate curriculum objectives.*

I.M. MARSH LIBRARY LIVERPOOL L17 6BD
TEL. 0151 231 5216/5299

# Introduction

The National Curriculum is now under review. After 2000 a new version of it will replace the 1988 original. *How should the aims of the revised curriculum be determined?*

That is the central question of this paper. It precedes questions about both the detailed structure of the curriculum and what specific aims should lie behind this. I will be saying something about both these matters in due course, but there is a danger in broaching them without prior consideration of our main question.

The danger is this. The National Curriculum provides the legal framework for nearly every child's school education – for all, that is, except those who are educated privately. It helps to shape the educational experience and later lives of all future citizens of England and Wales. As such, it is a powerful institution. If it gets things seriously wrong, its potential for harm is massive. That is why great care should be taken to ensure that its aims and the more specific curriculum objectives which derive from them are as well worked-out as possible.

It plainly would not do for the policy-makers who are to frame the national curriculum to begin by laying down a set of aims according to their *own* views about what is desirable. For if they did, then why should *their* value-preferences prevail? Why should the lives of so many millions of people be shaped according to the personal value-judgments of a small group of people?

The problem here concerns what I shall call *sectionalism*: the situation whereby some section of the population determines what the aims and broad contours of the school curriculum should be. The general question here is: why should any section of the population have the power to shape what the school experience and its aftermath should be for everyone else? What could give them the moral right to do so?

Of course, it might turn out that one section or another *does* have that moral right. Perhaps government policy-makers have some special knowledge or ability that entitles them to make pronouncements about the aims of education. Or perhaps some other group – teachers, say, or parents, or university academics – are in a better position than other people to do so. We simply do not know, short of investigating the topic, whether there is indeed some section or other which the rest of us can trust to make responsible decisions, or whether no version of sectionalism will do and we shall have to start elsewhere.

*That* is why – to come back to the main topic of this paper – the first question that has to be tackled in the current review of the National Curriculum is: how are its aims to be determined? This methodological question must be prior. If it is not, and whoever is in a position to influence events begins to lay down aims and more specific objectives, the questions immediately arise: why *their* aims? what gives *them* the right? – and these questions bring us back at once to the methodological issue.

# Before 1988 and after

The main weakness of the 1988 National Curriculum is that it was introduced as a reaction to one type of unjustified sectionalism, only to put another type in its place.

Before 1988 maintained schools were, in theory at least, able to determine what their aims and curricula should be. I say 'in theory', because in fact they were constrained in all sorts of ways, not least, as far as secondary schools went, by the requirements of public examinations. They had had this theoretical power for between 40 and 60-odd years, the curriculum of secondary grammar schools having been freed from state control in 1945, and that of elementary schools in 1926 (White 1975). From the 1960s onwards politicians and others began increasingly to question this power. They began to talk of 'the secret garden of the curriculum' – in which only teaching professionals, not the wider public, were allowed to wander. Callaghan's Ruskin College speech of 1976, in which professional control of the curriculum was directly challenged, was followed by moves, first by the then Labour government and after 1979 by its Conservative successors, towards greater and greater government involvement, culminating in the Educational Reform Act of 1988 which introduced the National Curriculum.

Before 1988, then, we find a section of the population, school teachers, who had the power to determine aims thrust upon them by the curriculum deregulations of 1926 and 1945. At no point in the history of those deregulations or later had there been an argued case for the wisdom of transferring curriculum power from state to teachers. Indeed, a well-founded case would have been hard to construct. Given the great influence which schools' curricula are intended to have on the lives of their pupils and therefore on the shape of future society, why should teachers have the power to set their broad contours, including their overall aims? True, there were – and are – good reasons why teachers should have considerable say at a more detailed level, that is, over the best routes, in the specific circumstances in which they are working, to reach more general objectives: only those close to the ground, like themselves, know what works best with these and these pupils in these and these situations. But this justifiable responsibility for curriculum specifics does not stretch to the power to set aims and broad curricular frameworks. Why should a section of the population have the power to help shape what future society should be like, when this was – as was becoming increasingly plain through the 1970s and 1980s – a power in which *every* citizen was equally entitled to participate? Just as generals were not entitled to decide on military policy, or tax-inspectors to lay down fiscal policy, so, it was felt, teachers did not have the right to determine educational policy. The content of the curriculum was a political, not a professional, matter and should be left, like other things in the political sphere including defence, foreign affairs and economic policy, within the remit of a democratically elected government.

After 1988 one form of sectionalism – teacher control of the curriculum – was replaced by another. Power shifted to the government. This meant in practice that those in control of education policy were able to institute the national curriculum they preferred with minimum consultation and regardless of obvious difficulties with it. Some say the 1988 National Curriculum originated with Mrs Thatcher's hairdresser, or with Kenneth

Baker's wife. But whoever it was, the nation speedily found itself yoked to the ten foundation and three core subjects with which we are now all familiar. Its social and economic future was now dependent on a mildly updated version of the secondary (ie grammar) school curriculum introduced after the Boer War. As for the aims of the maintained school's curriculum, including the National Curriculum, these occupied just two lines of the 1988 Educational Reform Act. They were to 'promote the spiritual, moral, cultural, mental and physical development of pupils at schools and of society; and prepare such pupils for the opportunities, responsibilities and experiences of adult life'. Not only was this new legal requirement placed on schools difficult to interpret – as, for instance, the millions of word-processed words on 'spiritual development' tapped out since 1988 testify. There was also no word on how these aims were supposed to provide a rationale for the foundation subjects. How were history, technology, mathematics and the rest supposed to contribute to spiritual, moral, cultural etc development? Nobody said in 1988; and nobody knows now.

## Can sectionalism be avoided?

The shift from professional control to control by a democratically elected government did not prevent sectionalism. It merely meant that a different section now held all the cards: the tiny group of politicians in charge of education policy in 1988 had replaced the much larger, though less cohesive, education establishment. What of the future? A new government is now in power. Will it take its own swing at the political football and change schools' aims according to its own preferences? If so, can it avoid replacing one set of sectional interests by another?

The School Curriculum and Assessment Authority (SCAA), now The Qualifications and Curriculum Agency (QCA), identified the purposes of education as a key area for future debate in January 1997, before the Labour government was elected. QCA has now launched a major drive in this area, seeking 'through a wide ranging consultation, general agreement on the aims of the school curriculum' (QCA, 1997). It has taken on board the widespread view that the 1988 aims were inadequate and insufficiently debated. It is looking for a 'coherent rationale', a 'clear statement' of aims for the curriculum as a whole and at each key stage, as well as an indication of how individual subject Orders may contribute to these.

All this is very welcome. The lesson of 1988 appears to have been learned. A fiat with next-to-no consultation is to be replaced, it seems, by a thought-through set of aims based on wide consensus. What role government ministers will play in any final resolution remains at present unclear. However things shake out, though, the central question remains. Can sectionalism be avoided? Will revised aims for the school curriculum be determined by a section of the population – government ministers, QCA officials in charge of the current consultation exercise, the constituencies consulted? If there is a change of government in a few years time, will power pass to another group or groups?

# A recent history of anti-sectionalism

The last 30 years have seen various attempts to avoid a kind of sectionalism. What can we learn from them?

I have written 'a kind of' sectionalism because the problem of bypassing sectional control of a *national* curriculum has been with us only very recently. But before 1988 schools still had curricula, if not national ones, and their aims and content had to be decided somehow. The problem of sectional control was still part of the educational scene. Where schools were in principle free to set their own curricula, what could stop headteachers or senior teachers with ideological bees in their bonnets or, more likely, an attachment to traditional ways of running things, from imposing such arbitrary curricular preferences on their schools? Was some *objective* basis for curriculum planning available?

## A CHILD-CENTRED CUL-DE-SAC

One route rightly attracted few followers, although it gave rise to a *cause célèbre* in the primary world in the 1970s. The teachers at William Tyndale school in Islington – and they were not alone – believed that *no* adult preferences about what should be learnt should be imposed on children. Children, *à la* Summerhill, were to be allowed to choose what they wished to learn – and if they wished to learn nothing, that, too, was up to them. This way of evading sectionalism fails because it equates young children with autonomous adults. It is indeed a basic principle in a liberal democratic society such as our own that people should – ideally – be self-directing in the conduct of their lives and that paternalist attempts to control what they do should be rejected. But this applies to adults, ie to those who are in theory equipped with the understanding they need in different areas to make important life choices. Children under 11 do not, by and large, have such understanding. They need a compulsory curriculum imposed upon them precisely to give them this.

## ACADEMIC EXPERTISE: ANOTHER DEAD-END?

A second way of coping with sectionalism looked more promising. This involved turning not to pupils, but to academic experts. If an objective basis for the curriculum was what was wanted, why not call on theorists of education? Psychologists and philosophers were pressed into service. The initiative did not always, by any means, come from them. Piaget's theory of cognitive development was a major anti-sectionalist resource in British primary education in the 1960s and later, but Piaget himself did nothing to put his theory to this use. In the 1990s Howard Gardner's theory of multiple intelligences has been taken over in a similar way, its author often expressing his surprise in print that the teaching world should have paid so much attention to it. In philosophy, the 1960s accounts by Richard Peters and Paul Hirst of 'worthwhile activities' and 'forms of knowledge' respectively were widely held, in some quarters, to provide the objective bedrock needed for curricular planning.

It is easy to understand how teachers and policy-makers, troubled by the power they have to shape others' lives, could turn so willingly to expertise based on the findings of empirical science or the ineluctabilities of logic. It is often hard for practitioners to assess the soundness of a favoured theory. When examined in detail, all the four theories just mentioned, as well as others of similarly guru-like stature, such as Chomsky's, prove to be unfounded. Piagetian psychology seems to avoid sectionalism because the directions in which children's minds develop are laid down, so it is held, by biology. It fails, because the biological model on which it rests, of an organism unfolding into more complex versions of itself at different stages, may apply well enough to plants and human bodies, but becomes incoherent when applied to human minds (Hamlyn, 1967). Howard Gardner's currently popular theory tells us that intelligence is not confined to the logico-mathematical sort tested by IQ tests, but is multiple, there also being seven (or more) other 'intelligences' – linguistic, musical, spatial, bodily-kinaesthetic, intrapersonal, interpersonal, and perhaps also naturalist and spiritual. It is not hard to see how those looking for an objective, science-based, taxonomy of the curriculum could be attracted to a view like this. Unfortunately for them, as with Piaget's theory prodding away at its foundations soon causes it to crumble. While the claim that intelligence is not only of the IQ variety but can take many forms is sound enough – the flexible adaptation of means to ends shown by the footballer being very different from that of the town-planner or travel-agent – there is no good reason for corralling these forms within Gardner's categories. A detailed examination of the criteria he relies on in this shows them to be deeply problematic (White, 1998).

Some of those unattracted by the aura of scientific respectability surrounding the psychologist have turned to the philosopher as the expert on educational aims. In the 1960s Richard Peters's writings persuaded many that a proper investigation of the concept of education revealed that it logically implied initiating pupils into 'worthwhile activities' to do with the pursuit of truth for its own sake in such domains as science, history, literature and philosophy (Peters 1966). Subsequent critique of this theory suggested that, far from giving an account of what education essentially involved, Peters seemed to be writing into his concept from the start his own predilection for a certain type of education, ie one founded on learning for its own sake. His colleague Paul Hirst's theory of a liberal education (Hirst, 1974) had, if anything, even more influence on teachers, the inspectorate and other policy-makers in the 1960s and 1970s. This, in some ways like Gardner's multiple intelligence theory, identified seven or eight logically distinct 'forms of knowledge or understanding': mathematics, physical science, human science, history, literature and the fine arts, philosophy, moral knowledge and possibly religious knowledge. Since a 'liberal education' required an induction into the different ways of thinking found in all these 'forms' – to be pursued not for instrumental reasons, eg to do with vocational choices, but solely, as with Peters, for their own sake, it is understandable how attractive this view could become for curriculum planners, especially those looking for dependable justifications of something like the traditional academic curriculum. Hirst's theory has long since bitten the academic dust. Even if – as is doubtful – all his separable forms of knowledge could be shown to exist, why should educational aims be built around these? Why should academic knowledge, especially when pursued for intrinsic reasons, be at the heart of education – rather than, say, character development, or equipping the pupil to lead a fulfilled and socially useful life? Hirst himself long ago jettisoned his early views in favour of an education closer to the 'social practices' of everyday – unacademic – life.

None of these leading psychological or philosophical theories have delivered the anti-sectionalist goods they seemed to promise. I realise that the sparseness of my critical comments on them, unavoidable in a short paper like this one, will leave many readers no option but to take what I have said on trust – and that this is a little paradoxical when my main point in this section has been that teachers and policy-makers have often had too much credence in 'experts'. I hope the references I have given to fuller critiques somewhat make up for this.

There is one good general reason why educational theory is unlikely to come up with the objective account of the curriculum that so many have sought. Educational theory aims at truth. This might make it seem ideally suited to provide the objectivity required, but this is an illusion. Psychologists investigate truths about how minds work; philosophers, about how concepts are interconnected and about the soundness of argumentation. But neither they nor any other educational theorists are experts on how to live, on what personal and communal flourishing consists in. Yet it is just this that lies at the root of the curriculum and its objectives. Here we are in the realm of values by which we should conduct our lives, no longer in that of psychological or logical facts. True enough, philosophers of education, perhaps more than most of their psychological colleagues, explore the world of values, looking for interconnexions and distinctions, and relating them to cultural horizons. But being good at understanding the moral virtues or the concept of well-being does not, notoriously, make them good at leading an ethically admirable life or able authoritatively to tell others how to lead one.

## THE APPEAL OF THE MARKET

Opponents of political control of the curriculum have sometimes seen the market as an alternative. This puts responsibility for basic decisions about aims and content in the hands of consumers, in this case families. Just as purchasers of groceries or furniture are better placed than others to decide what they want, so parents are – by and large – in the best position to know what kind of education is right for their children. In a market-based alternative to the present system, they would be able to choose from an array of schools – perhaps within a maintained sector, perhaps all private – the one whose orientation best suited their child. They would all need adequate information about the options. This could come from the publication of test scores and exam results and from other sources. Families who were still inadequately equipped to judge could be given tailor-made consumer guidance, perhaps on the *Which?* model.

This would avoid the dangers of sectionalism which could arise with a national curriculum – dangers we have seen exemplified in 1988. It would also avoid the sectionalism of professional control. Schools would still set their own curricular agenda, but unlike the pre-1988 version of professional control, they would not be able to *impose* this agenda on pupils and their families against their will.

Although the market solution avoids some forms of sectionalism, it does not prevent all. For one section of the population is still making the crucial decisions about aims: families. In effect, given the point made above that young children are not in a position to decide their own curriculum, this means parents. Why should these key decisions be left to parents? If they had some authoritative insight into the best life for their children to follow, there would be reason to do so. But just being a parent does not give one this equipment. Educational theorists, as we have seen, are not experts on the good life; and neither are parents.

Parental sectionalism excludes all non-parents from participating in decisions about aims. It also excludes parents from participating in decisions affecting other parents' children. This offends against the view that as citizens we all have some interest in the future flourishing of our political community. It is hard to see how this could be satisfied without our each having some input into how the next generations are to be brought up.

Parents may have strong views, of course, about how they want their children to be educated. Religious parents may want a particular sort of religiously based schooling; pacificists a pacifist one. But why should the parents' preferences be paramount? All this brings us back to an ambiguity in the market model. It is based on the principle of consumer sovereignty, in educational provision as in buying groceries. But who is the consumer in the former case? Is it the family, or the child? Plainly the person undergoing school education is the child. In some respects, where he or she is not in a position to make autonomous choices, parents act as proxy. It is they who decide where their children are to live; when the children are very young, it is they who decide what food they will eat or what clothes they will wear. But can they act as proxy when we turn from basic needs to more global concerns about how life should be lived? If we assume that when full citizens of a liberal-democratic society, children should be able

I.M. MARSH LIBRARY LIVERPOOL L17 6BD
TEL. 0151 231 5216/5299

to decide for themselves on the major contours of their lives, parents should not put obstacles in the way of this self-directedness. In so far as steering their children towards narrow, mind-closing, visions of the good life constitutes such an obstacle, young people need protection against the prejudices of their parents.

## LOOKING FOR CONSENSUS

A more promising way of avoiding sectionalism would seem to be to seek agreement about aims across the whole community. This way, all major constituencies would have a voice and none would be left out. Parents, for example, could have an input and so could teachers, other educational professionals and local authorities. The business community might have a say. Religious groups, minority cultural communities and other constituencies could also be included.

This broad approach – not necessarily based on the categories just instanced – is currently being adopted by QCA. Its recent statement on *Aims for the School Curriculum 5-16* (QCA, 1997) says that there needs to be much more explicitness about what schools should be doing.

QCA will therefore seek, through a wide-ranging consultation, general agreement on the aims of the school curriculum. In particular these will include

- a clear statement of generally accepted aims for the school curriculum, both as a whole and, more precisely, for each key stage;

- an indication of how the National Curriculum, including individual subject Orders and other statutory requirements, may contribute to these overall and key stage aims.

As part of this programme, QCA recently sent a questionnaire to all schools, to be returned by December 1 1997, asking them for their views on aims for the school curriculum Key Stages 1-4. It has also run invited seminars on the topic for representatives from headteachers, from primary schools and from secondary schools. Other initiatives include collecting accounts of educational aims in other countries and proposed consultations with parents, pupils and members of the business community.

QCA intends to submit a report on the outcomes of these various consultations to the Secretary of State for Education by April 1998. QCA will thus not be feeding the outcomes directly into policy changes at school level, as its predecessor SCAA did following its earlier attempt to reach consensus, this time on moral values.

In 1996 SCAA set up a National Forum for Values in Education and in the Community. This consisted of 150 people, 'most of whom were nominated by national organisations with concern for young people or education. It included representatives from the teaching profession, school governors, parents, teacher trainers, principal religions, academics, the legal professions, the media, youth workers and employers' (SCAA, 1996). One of its main remits was to give guidance to SCAA on 'to what extent there is any agreement on the values, attitudes and behaviour that schools should promote on society's behalf' (ibid). The Forum soon found that there was considerable agreement among its members about such common values. In its report these covered four areas: society, relationships, the self and the environment and included such things as truth, human rights, democratic participation, respect for others' dignity, cooperativeness, self-understanding, valuing the natural world as a source of wonder and inspiration. Members disagreed about the source of such values, some locating these in God, others in human nature, yet were able to reach consensus on the values themselves. In early 1997, according to SCAA's Chief Executive Nick Tate and Marianne Talbot, the SCAA consultant charged with taking forward the work of the National Forum, the fact 'that the values identified by the Forum are values upon which everyone of goodwill will agree was conclusively established by SCAA in a consultation that included a MORI omnibus poll of 1500 adults. Approximately 95 per cent of those with whom we consulted agreed to the values outlined in the Forum's statement' (Talbot and Tate, 1997:3)

As a result of these surveys of opinion, inside and outside the Forum, SCAA decided to build its guidance to schools on the spiritual, moral, social and cultural development for which it was responsible under the 1988 Education Reform Act 'around the values outlined in the Forum's statement' (p.9). It also recommended to schools that they use this statement to 'instil confidence in the existence and importance of shared values' (p.9). It is in this way that SCAA's search for shared values has been translated directly into policy decisions.

As stated earlier, QCA's search for consensus on the aims of the school curriculum will eventuate in a report for the Secretary of State rather than direct policy changes at school level. It is not clear yet how the Secretary of State will use the information he is given.

How far is the consensus-seeking approach a sound basis for any policy decisions the Secretary of State may wish to make? Are there lessons to be learnt from the SCAA exercise on values applicable to the QCA exercise on aims?

Consensus-seeking is plainly rooted in democratic soil. It is an attempt to prevent sectional control by a wide canvassing of opinion across the community. If intended to generate policy rather than mere background information, it faces, however, several difficulties. These can be illustrated in some cases from the SCAA values exercise.

### Adieu sectionalism?

The SCAA project on values sought a broad agreement across the whole community. How far did it achieve this by its two-stage system of seeking consensus within the 150-strong Forum on Values and then testing the Forum's agreed values by a public opinion poll? There are several points in this process at which sectional interests are likely to have influenced outcomes.

First, the 150 members of the Forum had to be selected. SCAA tells us, as stated above, that it 'included representatives from the teaching profession, school governors, parents, teacher trainers, principal religions, academics, the legal professions, the media, youth workers and employers'

(SCAA, 1996:4). The first thing that strikes one about this list is the heavy weighting towards the educational world. Why? If 1988 is supposed to have put the era of professional control behind us on the grounds of sectionalism, one would have expected a Forum more representative of the whole body of citizens. Where the Forum members *do* go beyond education is in the direction of religion, employers, lawyers and the media. Again, why? Are people in these areas supposed to have a clearer insight into the world of ethical values than the rest of the population? In many cases this would seem laughable. Two notable exclusions from this 'representative section of society' are the employed rather than employers, and the non-employed, including the retired.

Second, once the Forum began to meet there must have been some way of managing its deliberations so as to eventuate in the neat, four-category list of values which was put out to the MORI pollsters. What part did SCAA officials and consultants play in this? How far did they regiment what must have been pretty diverse and diffuse data into more manageable categories unconsciously reflecting their own value-preferences?

The QCA exercise on aims is also consulting widely across the community. Questionnaires have been sent to all schools; headteachers have been canvassed; plans are afoot (in November 1997) to involve parents, pupils and employers. Similar questions about the representativeness of this survey arise as arose over the SCAA project. There is no sign, as yet, that the mass of the population – in the shape of people employed in the non-educational sector, plus the large ranks of the unwaged – will be asked for *their* views on the aims of education. As with SCAA, too, the collating task facing QCA officials provokes questions about how unconscious bias will be prevented.[2]

### The HCF problem

The consensus-seeking approach takes it as read that there is unlikely to be universal agreement on all points. On some items there will be disagreement, on others agreement. The point of seeking consensus is to identify the latter. This means that only the least controversial items – as it were the highest common factor in the responses – will be included. This may lead to a bland set of aims, some of them perhaps couched in highly general language hiding radical differences of interpretation. Suppose, for instance, some respondents favour the promotion of personal self-directedness, while others believe that pupils should learn to be submissive to God's commands. Both aims could well be excluded. At the same time all parties might be able to agree with the scarcely disputable claim that schools should 'provide an excellent education for all young people' (to take the first item in the list of official national goals for schools in Australia).

Without knowing full details of the SCAA consultation exercise on values, one cannot say how far similar processes were at work there. But it is noteworthy that personal self-directedness did not figure in its list of agreed values. This is a key value in liberal thinking and one to which the overwhelming majority of people in a society like modern Britain are attached, at least to some extent. Most of us, that is, take it as read that individuals should be allowed and encouraged to decide on their major goals in life, their relationships and other attachments: we are far from a more tradition-directed society where one has no choice over whom one will marry, what sort of work one will do, where one will live, whom one will worship, and so on. Despite its prevalence in our society, this value was not caught within SCAA's net. Or could it be that it was somehow incorporated in the item 'trying to discover meaning and purpose in life'? Was this something which secular liberals could read in terms of self-directedness – to do with people seeking their own purposes in life; while religious believers could interpret it in terms of looking for divine purpose and meaning?

To come back to the QCA initiative on aims. Unless there are safeguards against this, the search for consensus may generate agreed formulations which, like the Australian example, cut little ice. The educational world is already familiar with this from schools' statements of aims which are couched so generally that they paper over conflicting viewpoints among staff members. This is an important point to make now that the 1988 National Curriculum is beginning to be rethought. The 1988 aims – about the promotion of spiritual, moral, cultural, mental and physical development, and about preparing pupils for the opportunities and responsibilities of adult life – were so general that they failed to indicate how they might be realized in more determinate objectives. Whatever revised aims come out of the QCA initiative must surely point in the direction of more specific aims in which they can be practically embodied.

Let me illustrate this point with one or two further examples taken from the QCA's survey of official aims from different countries. New Zealand calls for programmes 'which enable all students to realize their full potential as individuals' – an aim echoed, in slightly different language (eg using the phrase 'full development') by Australia, Italy, Japan, Singapore and Spain. All these countries give this aim pride of place. But what *is* it for all students to realize their full potential? Does it mean that a child adept, as many children are, at, say, doing elementary mathematics, playing a team game and painting passably interesting pictures should be encouraged to go as far *as she possibly can* in all these fields? If so, how could one justify this? It seems to cut across the individual's own autonomy to decide which talents she wishes to develop to the hilt, if any; which she wishes to foster to some extent; and which she prefers to let fade. Again, should we assume that pupils *do have* a 'full potential' in one or more fields? This looks as though it implies there are *ceilings* on what they can achieve. Is this something we should accept? What evidence is there for it – or against it?

This 'full development' or 'full potential' aim crumbles at a touch. Despite its venerability in educational circles – its liability to be trotted out on any aims-listing occasion, whether by a primary school headteacher or by a framer of a national curriculum – a mild subjection of it to logical analysis reveals it to be pretty meaningless. It does not point in any particular direction when it comes to realizing it more determinately. That is because it is not *meant* to be be so realized. It is not intended to cut curricular ice. Rather, it finds its place at the top of aims lists because it seems acceptable to all and it has traditionally been taken as read as belonging there, with no one prepared to question it.

Contrast this aim with another from Australia's list: 'to provide students with an understanding and respect for Australia's cultural heritage, including the particular cultural background of Aboriginal and ethnic groups'. No doubt there are problems here of interpreting how this is to be applied. 'Understanding cultural heritage' can be taken in different ways. But at least with this aim there is some sense of direction. It points to a kind of attainment which can be specified – and argued about – in more detail. Its users know how to go on in a way closed to them with the 'full potential' aim. Those responsible for revising the aims of the British National Curriculum should make them of the former sort, not the latter.

The second difficulty with the consensus-seeking approach, then, is the temptation to produce general statements whose acceptability to all parties increases as a function of growing emptiness of content and consequent insusceptibility of application. At the same time, controversial positions tend to be winnowed out whatever their well- or ill-foundedness. The soundness of arguments for or against different views will be discounted in favour of counting heads.

### List or logic?

At every level, all the agreed accounts of aims I have seen have taken the form of *lists*, in which the logical relationships between items and categories included are left unexplored. This is true, for instance, of the objectives of the foundation subjects in the 1988 curriculum as laid down by the subject working parties. At the other end of the range it is true of the official aims of different national school systems. The SCAA values, too, appeared as lists of unrelated items in four categories.

The reason why consensus-seeking is likely to end up in lists is obvious. It is easier to agree on a form of words than on a rationale – a rationale likely to relate to other items. We have touched on the point already. The SCAA Forum was able to agree that 'trying to discover meaning and purpose in life' is a core value. No indication is given of *why* this is held to be important or how it is supposed to relate to other items in the same category like 'develop a sense of self-worth' or 'try to understand our own character, strengths and weaknesses'. *Prima facie*, these three items would appear to be logically connected in some way, but since no gloss is given, no one can say.

Again, being satisfied with a mere list avoids problems over prioritization. The National Curriculum objectives for history laid down by the History Working Group after 1988 were presented as a list. Some items had to do with aims intrinsic to the subject to do with arousing interest in the past, disciplined enquiry etc; while others were about pupils' sense of identity, cultural roots and shared inheritances. School history tends to be riven between those who value its learning for intrinsic reasons and those favouring its contribution to personal and social education. Presenting a list of items in no hierarchical order enabled the Working Group to do justice to both points of view without having to make a commitment on which aims are more important than others. This is another possible danger which the QCA initiative should bear in mind.

### The problem of authority

Some of the difficulties raised above could in principle be averted. Care could be taken to sound out a more comprehensive cross-section of the population than in the cases cited; and the work of officials who have to discipline a mass of information into a few categories could itself be impartially monitored. General statements of little practical applicability, intended to paper over cracks between disputed positions, could be banned and only aims susceptible of more determinate realization could be allowed. (To be fair to the SCAA value enquiry, many of its principles of action do fall into the second category – eg that society should 'help people to know about the law and legal processes', or that we should 'repair habitats devastated by human development wherever possible'.) Mere listing of aims would not be enough: agreed reasons would have to be given for the items presented and priorities among them established.

Even if these improvements were made – and the practical difficulty of making them should not be underestimated – there would still be a logical difficulty about building a policy recommendation on the basis of such a consensus. The latter would yield an empirical *fact* – that x per cent of the population believe that such and such hierarchically arranged aims should guide the work of schools for such and such reasons. But what policy makers need to know is what *should* be done, or what it is *best* to do, on the basis of this fact. Why should one believe that a survey of opinion should reveal, not only what people *think* is right, but what *is* right? Suppose 95 per cent of the British population turned out to favour capital punishment: would that make capital punishment the right policy to follow?

The problem is an instance of the general problem that there seems to be a logical gap between statements of empirical fact and ethical statements about what is best or about what ought to be done.

Can this problem be overcome? Not, I believe, by remaining within the framework of consensus-seeking. Any revision of the aims of the National Curriculum must start from a different point.

# Towards a new National Curriculum

The last section reviewed several attempts to avoid sectionalism in the determination of school aims and found them all wanting. The imposition of sectional aims cannot sensibly be bypassed by opposing *any* imposition of aims on pupils and letting the latter decide their own agenda. Appeals to academic 'expertise' in the hope of locating objective aims are also problematic, as are also recourse to market forces and parental rights, or a search for consensus across the community.

So where do we go from here if we still want to avoid sectionalism? Of all the alternatives just reviewed, the search for consensus best points the way forward. We should recall yet again the main reason why a National Curriculum is preferable to curricula under the professional control of heads and teachers. This is the democratic reason that every citizen, and not only a section of the citizenry like the body of professional educators, should have the right to participate in socially important decisions such as what the aims of school education ought to be. The search for cross-community consensus is an attempt to see that the views of as many citizens as possible are represented. It is rooted, therefore, and rightly, in an attachment to democratic principles.

The consensus approach founders in the end on its inability to get beyond empirical facts about people's preferences to ethical value judgements about what to do. But in reality the ethical value judgement it needs to generate policy decisions has already been taken on board. In seeking ideally to encompass the views of every citizen, it is committed to the worthwhileness of democracy itself. This raises the interesting question: if we assume from the outset that democracy is a good thing, how far can we generate from this assumption more determinate democratic values, which in turn can generate the aims of a national education system? Moreover, how far can we generate these values *directly* – without taking the longer route via consensus-seeking?[3]

## DEMOCRATIC VALUES

Let us see what mileage there is in this new suggestion – and what pitfalls. As we have seen, political control of the aims and content of education via a national curriculum is preferable to professional or other sectional control because of the democratic assumption that all citizens and not only some should be able to participate in important decisions affecting the shape of their society in the future. The basic rationale for the British National Curriculum assumes that democratic principles are desirable. Not everyone would be happy with this assumption. Some believers in a theocratic state might not be; neither would those who favour oligarchy or autocracy. In the context of this paper we need not argue the full case for or against democracy against its opponents. That is because well-grounded commitment to a national curriculum brings with it commitment to democracy. We can take it as read that all parties discussing the central issue of this paper – about how the aims of the British National Curriculum are to be revised – will go along with this commitment. The question most immediately facing us is not: is democracy justified?, but: what is involved in this 'democracy' to which we are all committed?

Identifying the question in this way may suggest that this new version of anti-sectionalism bids fair to receive as short shrift as all the others. For what is there to guarantee that all parties in the debate will understand the term 'democracy' in the same way? We made some play above with the point that recourse to bland, general terms can paper over cracks between different views. May not the same be true here? The concept of democracy has been hotly contested in political philosophy. Some would identify it with certain *procedures* – eg regular elections or majority rule – even if those procedures lead to political power being always in the hands of a dominant group or competing elites. Others would argue that such dominance is at odds with the principle that each individual is of equal intrinsic value, which generates the notion that the rights of minorities need to be protected. On this second view, democratic *values* are at the root of the concept, and democratic procedures can only be understood in the light of these. A second fracture line between competing views of democracy separates those who accept some form of representative system as necessary for a highly populated modern state and those who favour the fully participatory system found originally in the Greek city state and realisable in modern conditions only by maximizing small-scale participatory arrangements in as many aspects of our lives as possible.

The contended nature of the concept of democracy does not scupper this new anti-sectionalist approach. For those who are party to the debate, accepting as they do the democratic rationale for a national curriculum, must already have a relatively determinate conception of democracy, one which ranges them on some sides of the fracture lines just mentioned and not others. They cannot be attached to procedures rather than values, for in the emphasis they put on anti-sectionalism they show their commitment to the democratic principle that each citizen should have equal power in making political decisions. They cannot deny that some kind of representative government is necessary, since in accepting that there should be a national curriculum and that some way must be found for determining its aims, how else could the views of all the citizens be taken into account, imperfectly as any representative system must admittedly be in this regard?

We can take it, then, that the democratic political system in question will be a representative one (which is not to rule out participation at all sorts of levels below the national one). It will also be one defined in terms of values rather than procedures. There are independent reasons for favouring these two conclusions, but I will not argue these here, partly for reasons of space but also for the *ad hominem* reason that there is no need, since all parties to the debate are *ipso facto* committed to them.

What more can we say about the democratic values, to which the parties are committed?

## POLITICAL EQUALITY

The principle that each citizen should have equal power in making political decisions is part of the principle of political equality. This is to be distinguished from more substantive principles of equality, for example that everyone should have the same income or minimum educational attainments. It rests on the fundamental ethical value, often associated with Kant, that each human being is of intrinsic value as a person – that he or she must always be treated as an end and never merely as a means. We may call this the ethical value of respect for persons (see Harrison, 1993, ch XV).

## PERSONAL AUTONOMY

Embedded in this ethical value is the assumption that individuals' flourishing matters. This brings in another root value in democratic thinking – the promotion and protection of personal well-being. What the principle of political equality adds to this is that *every* citizen's well-being is *equally* important.

We can take it, therefore, that all sides will agree that democracy has to do with promoting and protecting the well-being of all citizens. Of course, not only democracies can have this aim. So could a benevolent dictatorship. What typifies democracy, at least in the modern age, is the extra dimension it gives to the notion of personal well-being. Even if a benevolent dictatorship worked successfully and impartially for the good of each, few among us could brook its paternalist assumption that it knew, often better than its subjects themselves, in what their personal flourishing consisted. Democracy works with a conception of the latter which assumes that it is individuals themselves who are to determine the major goals and relationships success in which enables them to lead a flourishing life. It embodies, in other words, the ethical value labelled 'self-determination' or 'personal autonomy'. We met this value above, when we noted its apparent absence from the SCAA Forum's list of agreed values. As was then pointed out, it is a key value in liberal thinking. In a tradition-directed society personal well-being is still a function of success in achieving one's major goals (including goals to do with relationships), but those goals are laid down for one by the mores of one's group or by religious or political authority. The notion that individuals *choose* their most significant goals has come with the growth of a liberal society over the last 300 years in this country and in others. Today virtually all of us take it as read that it is up to us whether we marry or not marry, that there is no direction of labour, that people are not debarred, as they were in the Soviet Union, from living in what town they like, and so on. A commitment to personal autonomy is at the heart of modern liberal democracy (Harrison, 1993, ch X). It is incorporated in the claim, discussed above, that each person should be equally entitled to participate in political decisions – for this claim rests on the notion of individuals collectively and freely choosing important – in this case political – goals whose attainment or non-attainment affects the well-being of them all.

## LIBERTY

Democracy, as we understand the term today, is a political system premised in part on the promotion and protection of the autonomous well-being of each citizen. It helps to provide some of the conditions without which autonomous flourishing would not be possible. Other polities – benevolent despotisms again, for example – can, with good fortune, ensure some of these: internal and external peace, physical necessities of life like food, clothing, shelter. What democracy uniquely tries to provide on top of these, partly through its specific kind of legal system, is the liberty of thought and action without which autonomous regulation of one's life would be impossible. The principle of liberty states that people should not be prevented from doing what they want by constraints imposed by people, unless harm to others is involved.

As with other values mentioned, there are qualifications to be made. Are there cases – perhaps an aspect of the compulsory use of seatbelts or the outlawing of drugs? – where liberty should rightly be constrained for the individual's own good? Are there cases – perhaps compulsory military service? – where liberty can rightly be infringed for the sake of some other, allegedly weightier, ethical consideration? For the purposes of this essay these qualifications are not as important as the identification of the core democratic value itself, despite its rough edges.

## CIVIC CONCERN FOR OTHERS' WELL-BEING

We can take it as read that any political system will have good reason to encourage some constraints on the naked pursuit of self-interest, for example through laws against damage to others' persons and property, or breach of contract. But a democratic system takes this further. It is as part of the notion that every citizen be enabled to participate in political decisions that a democratic system values cooperation among individuals for common ends. Its concept of the citizen is of a person whose well-being is entwined in this respect with the well-being of others – even though on occasions it can be at odds with this. It is possible, perhaps, for an autonomous person to flourish as an egoist who has no interest in others' flourishing. But that kind of personal autonomy is not one which a democratic regime could favour. A democratic system of government presupposes a political community, one in which this intertwining of individuals' well-being will occur at different levels where democratic decision-making is found. Democracy expects and requires a certain type of personal character in its citizens. They must care about the well-being of other people, not only those with whom they have face-to-face relationships, but also those unencountered 'strangers' in the community and beyond its borders whose fate matters to them too. Autonomous work is one of the ways in which this care is manifested.

Again, there are further issues here which would need to be explored in a fuller account and which are more controversial. How close, for instance, does the political community in question come to a *national* community? Can national sentiment be detached from chauvinism and be seen, benignly, as Isaiah Berlin (see Gray 1995), David Miller (1995) and other political philosophers have argued, as providing the affective, communal background necessary for a liberal democratic state? How far should democratic principles and procedures be instituted sub-nationally at the level of, for example, the workplace?

Although there will be differences of opinion about these and other matters, I think we can take it that the more general notion of civic concern will be acceptable to all those who accept a democratic framework as a basis for national curriculum planning.

## KNOWLEDGE

Knowledge is important to every kind of political system. Rulers will want their decisions to be well-informed. This is as true of autocrats and oligarchs as of democrats. In addition to the necessary knowledge within the capability of the rulers themselves, every system of government needs expertise on which to rely. To that extent a democracy, like any other polity, must ensure the existence of a reliable body of experts in different domains. In our modern age it is dependent on sophisticated forms of knowledge, especially in the natural and economic sciences, unknown to previous societies. As in other polities, rulers in a democracy must be in a position to draw on this expertise in making political decisions. This implies some understanding on their part, not of the fine detail of the specialisms, but of the larger bearing of their findings on political arrangements. It also implies a readiness not to take everything that experts say on trust, but to submit their claims to some kind of independent assessment.

Since in a democracy it is ultimately citizens who are the rulers, it follows that they will need two kinds of knowledge or understanding: that within the capability of non-experts, for example a basic understanding of the voting system or an elementary grasp of the principles of economic policy-making; and some knowledge of the relevance of expert knowledge to political decision-making and some understanding of how the reliability of experts can be checked. (On knowledge as a democratic value, see Harrison, 1993, ch IX.)

We have now identified a number of values required for modern liberal democracy – political equality, the promotion and protection of autonomous well-being, liberty of thought and action, civic concern for other people's welfare, knowledge. There may be others. In a longer work there is much more that should be said in defence and elaboration. But what has been said so far is probably enough for our present purposes. That is because the main focus of this essay is methodological. It seeks to answer the question: how should the aims of the revised national curriculum be determined? Its positive proposal is that these should be derived from the commitment to democratic values which all supporters of the idea of a national curriculum should rationally accept. In the brief sketch which is all it can provide, it can only point to some core democratic values and show how these generate aims of education at different levels of specificity. It is this *direction* of thought that is important – from a commitment to democracy, to its underlying values, to general aims of education, to more specific curriculum objectives. People may, I hope, agree about this general framework even though they disagree on elements within it: on just what the core values of democracy are, on how they are to be qualified, on the aims derivable from them and so on down to curriculum details.

With this in mind, let us now see how the values picked out above can generate aims and curricula. This will exemplify the direction of thought just mentioned.

## GENERATING EDUCATIONAL AIMS

The further one moves from underlying values towards general aims of education and thence towards more determinate curricular goals, the more room there will be for differences of view. In what follows, although my aim is methodological, I shall have to *illustrate* the direction in which thought can proceed by more substantive, more concrete proposals. As I see it, some of these, at the more general level, are likely to be broadly acceptable to all parties. At more specific levels, for example the content and structure of the timetabled curriculum, there are very many ways of operationalizing higher-level considerations. All I can do here is give one or two examples of how the latter *may* be cashed out. My intention is not to lay down prescriptions.

The point that as one gets more determinate, flexibility of routes to the same general goals increases, bears on the question: where, along this gamut, should statutory national curriculum prescriptions end? The general criterion for this should now be familiar. The argument for political rather than professional control of the curriculum only applies to the broad framework of values and goals, not curricular specifics. Citizens have an interest in the former because it bears closely on the shape of the future political community itself. The more one moves towards specifics, the more case there is for professional control. At the most determinate levels teachers *do* have an expertise which they lack over the question: where should our society be going? Only they know what best routes to follow in the light of what particular groups of children already know, how they can best be motivated, what their own teaching strengths are, and a host of other factors.

At the beginning of what follows, we will still plainly be operating in the sphere of political control. Later points belong to a greyer area.

My main task will be to show that the values we are dealing with, even the highest-level ones, *do give us a direction* for working out specifics. To illustrate this, I shall begin with knowledge as a democratic value. Not that it is the most important such value – on the contrary, as I will try to show. It was argued above that every citizen needs to be equipped with politically relevant knowledge of a non-expert sort and some understanding of the bearing of expert knowledge on politics and of how experts' reliability can be assessed. Further specification of this will be necessary of course, but one can already see how the argument points, among other things, towards some understanding of the larger contours of one's society against their historical horizons, of the workings of the constitution, of basic economics, of current affairs nationally and globally – once again with a historical dimension, of the political relevance of science, technology, mathematics, economics as a science, medicine etc. In this way we make contact with some of the elements in the existing National Curriculum – although other items just mentioned are absent from it.

Although knowledge is of enormous importance, it is not the *first* value on which we should be concentrating. That is because it is a derivative democratic value, not a basic one. The fundamental notions of democracy are that each person is of equal intrinsic importance, as both ruler and ruled; and that each person's autonomy should be protected and promoted, both as an individual and more specifically as a participant in political decision-making. These values require dispositions of concern for the well-being of other citizens on the part of each. Given all these values, it *follows* that the autonomous citizen needs politically relevant knowledge like that described above.

He or she also needs knowledge of other kinds and for other purposes. We will come to that in a moment. For more basic than knowledge aims are aims to do with attitudes and dispositions. The democratic citizen must have accepted – not merely in an intellectual sense, but as guides to his or her behaviour – the fundamental values of political equality, autonomy, liberty and civic concern for others. We can put this in terms of the personal qualities or, in an older terminology which is now coming back into use the 'virtues of character', which citizens should possess. These will include such things as respect for all persons as ends in themselves, including self-respect; self-directedness; tolerance; benevolence and non-maleficence; cooperativeness in the pursuit of common ends – at work and elsewhere; moral courage. Self-directedness brings with it further personal qualities or virtues: whole-hearted commitment to one's major projects and relationships; independence of judgment; self-confidence; self-understanding. The wider value of personal well-being, of which autonomous well-being is a modern variant, also depends on such traditional virtues as courage in the face of different kinds of physical fear; proper control of one's bodily appetites for food, drink and sex; self-control in relation to anger; patience, and so on.

These are some of the personal qualities which democratic citizenship requires. It is not a complete inventory, but it is already beginning to burgeon into a lengthy list. What is noteworthy about it is that it is *practically helpful*, meaning by this that it gives some guidance as to what dispositions parents and schools can help to foster in children. As a list, if this is metaphorically allowable, it has teeth. In this it is a world away from the *practically useless* first aim of the 1988 National Curriculum about spiritual, moral, social and mental development.

Methodologically, then, this is the first stage in determining the aims of a revised National Curriculum: to identify the desirable personal qualities and attitudes which need to be cultivated in children. Of course, this is not only a task for the school curriculum: it applies as much to the upbringing that parents provide, and perhaps to the media as well. The next step, methodologically, is to see what dispositions like those mentioned entail in the way of further desirable attainments.

Because the personal qualities are already so many, a full discussion of this would take more space than I have here. (For an account of personal values and curricular implications, see White 1990.) Again, I shall proceed by giving one or two examples, so as to indicate how curriculum planning should proceed at this point.

There is growing interest these days in the education of the emotions. Daniel Goleman's (1996) new book *Emotional Intelligence* is a best seller.

The new British pressure group *Antidote* has as its first main goal 'enabling people to develop the emotional and social skills they need if they are to manage their lives in ways that benefit themselves and our society' (*Antidote* 1997). Several of the personal qualities mentioned above point in this direction. Children need to learn how to regulate their emotional life, so that it supports and does not hinder their own and others' well-being. They need to manage their fear, anger, anxiety, feelings of shame, guilt and pride, sympathies, contempt and hatred, feelings of attachment and love. Above all, they need to become motivated in time by different forms of love – sexual love, friendship, the wider civic friendship which binds them to others in their political community, commitment to self-chosen projects. The foundations of emotional education should be laid, of course, in the family, but the school's role here is also crucial.

I have mentioned knowledge and understanding in connexion with the role of citizen-ruler and will not repeat the kinds of learning this involves. But the cultivation of personal qualities brings with it further knowledge requirements. Take self-directedness. This entails choosing one's major goals and relationships autonomously rather than conforming to custom or authority. Autonomous choice requires an adequate array of options from which selection can be made. The educational implication is that young people have to be brought up to understand such arrays of options so as to be in a position to choose or reject them. The options cover a multitude of fields – jobs, non-vocational interests, life-styles, religious affiliations, types of relationship etc. Young people need to know about ranges of work open to them; intellectual, artistic, and sporting activities; types of sexual and non-sexual relationship; and much more. This ties in directly with the widely held aim of schooling to do with 'opening up options' or 'widening horizons'. It is not difficult to see how some traditional curriculum elements – science and the arts, for instance – have an essential role in this story. Without some grasp of science and mathematics, so many jobs would be out of one's reach; without some feeling for the arts, one would be deprived of what for many people becomes a major constituent of their well-being. These are only two examples, of course.

LIVERPOOL JOHN MOORES UNIVERSITY
LEARNING SERVICES

As well as understanding what different options involve, young people also need some insight into the kind of society through which they will be threading their self-directed path. We have already encountered learning about one's society in connexion with one's specifically civic role. We can now add that this same desideratum follows from the more personal ideal of self-directedness.

Other personal qualities mentioned also bring with them demands on knowledge. Proper regulation of one's physical desires requires some understanding of sex, bodily health, dietary science, drug addiction. Self-knowledge and altruistic virtues like benevolence or friendship depend on psychological awareness – although whether academic psychology is as reliable a vehicle for this as literature or personal interaction is a further question.

Again, all this only gives a partial picture of the knowledge and understanding which children will need. A fuller account would map this more systematically. It would also say more about the logical hierarchies among knowledge which now come into view, for example the dependence of knowledge about society on some grasp of science and technology; the key role of literacy in the acquisition of so much else.

## FROM AIMS TO CURRICULA

So much for a brief sketch of some of the aims of education generated by democratic values, with aims to do with personal qualities in the van and knowledge aims derived from these. Methodologically, the next stage is to work out how such aims should be realized in institutional arrangements. I will give the barest sketch of these, partly because this has been spelt out in much more detail in the IPPR publication *A National Curriculum for All*, which Philip O'Hear and I wrote in 1991.

## FAMILIES

Much of the early groundwork will be laid by families. As the child's first educators, it is the parents' job to begin to nurture desirable personal qualities, teach children language, equip them with elementary knowledge about the social and natural worlds, start the job of extending horizons. How far guidelines, or forms of parental education, would help them to see the links between these familiar tasks and wider educational aims is a matter which could merit exploration.

## SCHOOLS AND FAMILIES

What part should the school play? The first point to make is that its work should not be sharply separated from that of the family. The underlying aims of both are the same and there is every reason for teachers and parents to keep closely in touch. The school builds on the foundations laid by the family. It develops personal qualities into more complex forms, informed increasingly by the new knowledge acquired in the classroom which children can now bring to them. Think, for instance, of the personal quality of benevolence. While it must be parents who first nurture sympathetic concern for others' well-being on the small, domestic scale of family-members, friends and pets, teachers can extend these sympathies towards 'strangers' in the larger national community and beyond, as well as to fictional and historical characters. This depends on the fuller knowledge that the child will now be acquiring of socio-economic arrangements, history, literature etc.

## WHOLE SCHOOL FEATURES

When considering the procedures which a school may adopt in order to realize larger aims, one should think first of whole school processes and only then of the timetabled curriculum.

The role of whole school practices in the cultivation of attitudes and personal qualities is now widely acknowledged. This is already often harnessed to the virtues and emotions needed for democratic citizenship and a revision of the National Curriculum could well systematize this further. Equality of respect, tolerance, concern for others, moral courage, personal independence, self-control can all be encouraged and celebrated through a school's formal and informal expectations, inside the classroom and beyond it.

## THE TIMETABLED CURRICULUM

Finally, to the timetabled curriculum. Knowledge aims, demanding structured teaching and learning, obviously come into their own here. They are not the only considerations. In the light of all that has been said, discussions, workshops and other activities in the area of PSHE (Personal, Social and Health Education) will be of great importance. So will activities to do with deepening enjoyment of the arts. But the acquisition of knowledge will also be a major feature. As I'm using the expression, this covers far more than fact-learning. It includes also an understanding of underlying principles as well as forms of know-how (eg to read, to write, to think historically, to operate a computer). Our derivation of knowledge aims from underlying ethical values pointed to desirable attainments in science, mathematics, history, technology, social science, politics, psychology, self-understanding, economics. Some of these are included in the present National Curriculum, others are not. Where they *are* included, there is a case for re-examining present statutory requirements to see whether they fit the new, democracy-driven, bill. Key Stage 3 History, for instance, at present covers the Norman Conquest to Hiroshima in effectively two and a half years, only a small fraction of which is devoted to the twentieth century. Many, possibly most, students do no more history before they leave school. How far should the balance be tilted more to an understanding of the last 100 years?

I need not go into further detail about the timetabled curriculum, since I am not issuing prescriptions but only indicating a thought-path. In any case, the detail can only be worked out once the superstructure of more general aims is more fully in place. As has been said, beyond a certain point – or, more likely, grey area – details should be left to the teachers. The democratic argument for political rather than professional control applies only to the general aims and broad curriculum framework. Beyond that, only professionals have the relevant expertise.

A key point to make about any remodelling of the timetabled curriculum is that it should be a harmonious mosaic in which the contribution of the most detailed items to the overall picture of educational aims can be clearly worked out by well founded patterns of justificatory argument. An even more important point to make is that the teachers who work within the system should also *be at home with* these justifications. They must see the specifics of what they do day to day as connected with their largest purposes. Shortfalls here have always been a weakness in the teaching profession, in Britain as elsewhere. The coming of the National Curriculum in 1988 could have helped to change things for the better, but its overprescriptiveness, coupled with the pressures of external assessment, has tended from all accounts to keep teachers' attention too firmly on required particularities.

# Conclusion

The chain of argument is now complete. We began with the question: how should the aims of a post-2000 National Curriculum be determined? A central obstacle here is sectionalism: the imposition of the value-preferences of one section of the population. Ways of avoiding the problem of sectionalism were explored and found wanting. These include the search for consensus about educational aims at present being undertaken by QCA. Consensus-seeking, however, provided a clue to what is a more adequate way of countering sectionalism: rooting any new National Curriculum in the underlying values of democracy itself, values which all those who accept the principle of a national curriculum may be expected to accept. These values were shown to generate general educational aims of several sorts, which in turn were shown to be capable of realization in more specific curriculum objectives. The emphasis throughout the argument has been methodological: to find a sound way of answering our initial question.

I.M. MARSH LIBRARY LIVERPOOL L17 6BD
TEL. 0151 231 5216/5299

This essay's conclusion, that aims need to be rooted in democratic values, challenges the claim of any particular government that the fact that it has been democratically elected gives it the right to lay down, or remodel, what the content of the National Curriculum shall be, according to its own political perspectives. The National Curriculum should not become a political football, the subject of whatever sectional preferences this or that Secretary of State might possess. Democratic rootedness goes deeper than this. It reaches the bedrock of the constitution itself.

Has the argumentation been persuasive? Have I strayed beyond my self-imposed methodological brief into the territory of prescriptions based on my own personal preferences? I have tried not to do so, but others may tell me if I have. Or they may not. We are on dangerous ground. Philosophers, including myself, are not authorities on the good life and hence on the aims of education. But sometimes they are taken by others to be just this. Claims made tentatively or merely illustratively may be taken as hard-and-fast truths. I need to make it plain that everything I have written here is up for grabs. The whole argument about sectionalism and democracy may be faulty. The list of democratic values is contestable. The further points about aims and curricula may be even more contentious. At best I hope I may have indicated, as I have said more than once, a general direction in which policy-makers can proceed. Further discussion about the more debatable issues can take place before things are set in statutory stone.

One last worry. Those who think of themselves as political realists will say that the remodelling of the curriculum in 2000 or later cannot be as root-and-branch as would seem to follow from the argument of this essay. Changes will have to be incremental, not revolutionary. Talk to the teachers, ask them, as some of those representing foundation disciplines have been asked in the recent QCA monitoring exercise, whether they want no change to the National Curriculum, slight change, or major change. Very few will go for the third of these: most have been too pressured by the choppings and changings of the last few years to want anything really radical.

It is not yet clear how thoroughgoing or conservative any remodelling will be. Some people are already saying how useful it would be to the government to have a 'big idea' for the remodelling of the curriculum. Perhaps this paper could sow a seed for this. On the other hand, after all the upheavals they have recently experienced it is understandable that teachers should not want major change – despite the serious objections they also often have to present prescriptions. I hope that the government will not take teachers' wishes as decisive. If it is inclined to do so, the logic of the argument about why a National Curriculum is desirable – about avoiding the sectionalism of professional interests – should make it reconsider. But perhaps, in any case, some way of overcoming resistance to yet another major change can be found. In objecting to it, teachers assume that it will make their work more burdensome. This was indeed true of the 1988 changes and of some later emendations. But suppose changes after 2000 were likely to make teaching *more fulfilling*. Would they then oppose them?

The very same teachers who want no more upheaval are often those who object to the minute control of their work that the 1988 National Curriculum introduced. If arguments like those in this paper are accepted, state control will be reined back. Instead of a national curriculum tough on minutiae but vacuous on aims, we shall have one with a well worked-out set of aims and a broad framework of statutory curricular requirements flowing from this, but which leaves the specifics to professional judgment. Most teachers may be expected to welcome the greater freedom this will give them. Those who need more support can be supplied with non-statutory guidance, which it is up to them to accept or reject. All teachers will become more autonomous in their work, less the instruments of an alien prescription. Given adequate in-service training in the fundamentals of the new system, they will be able to connect the particularities of their day-to-day work with the very widest purposes of education. They will be able, collectively and individually, to give sound justifications of what they do in terms of higher-level considerations. They will no longer feel alienated by having to serve the purposes of an incoherent system. They will feel at home in an enterprise in which they have part-ownership as autonomous professionals. As such, they will act as more acceptable role-models for their students.

They will teach them by their own example what it means to be a democratic citizen.

If the National Curriculum changes in this direction, more will have to go. The present system of national assessment, not least. To pursue this in detail would take me even further from the methodological brief of this paper. I will only say that the purposes of assessment need as thorough a re-examination as the purposes of the curriculum itself. Two types of assessment that need to be firmly separated are these. On the one side, formative assessment designed solely to help pupils learn. On the other, a way of evaluating the work of a school to ensure that it is working well and that local parents can have confidence in it. Neither of these need have anything to do with the byzantine scheme of national assessment which is the cause of so many of our troubles.

## Notes

1.    I am grateful to my colleagues Richard Aldrich, Steve Bramall and Patricia White and to Ian Colwill and Chris Jones of the QCA National Curriculum Review team for their very helpful comments on an earlier draft.

2.    The QCA National Curriculum Review team has been scrupulous in foreseeing this difficulty and taking steps to cope with it. It has commissioned a research group from Manchester University under Dr Bill Boyle of the Centre for Formative Assessment Studies at the School of Education to produce a data-driven classification of school responses to the QCA questionnaire on their views about aims and priorities at the different key-stages.

3.    The idea that the school curriculum should be based on democratic values has not, needless to say, originated with this paper. Twenty-five years ago, Patricia White spelt out a cogent argument on partly similar lines in her 'Education, Democracy and the Public Interest' in R.S. Peters (ed.) *The Philosophy of Education,* Oxford: Oxford University Press ,1973. She filled out her ideas further in her book *Beyond Domination: an essay in the political philosophy of education,* London: Routledge & Kegan Paul, 1983.

# 2
# A Curriculum
# for the Nation

**RICHARD ALDRICH**
Professor of History of Education
Institute of Education University of London

## ABSTRACT

*Two questions are addressed in this paper. The first is: what are the
main strengths and weaknesses of common curricula in general and of
the National Curriculum in particular? The second, given that the
aims and content of school curricula have been debated for centuries,
is: what lessons may be drawn from an historical perspective upon
these issues? In considering this latter question particular emphasis is
placed upon the writings of John Locke, the seventeenth-century
political and educational thinker.*

# Introduction

The National Curriculum is to be revised for the twenty-first century. As part of that revision process the Qualifications and Curriculum Authority (QCA) has declared 'that there is a need to develop a much clearer statement about the aims and priorities of the school curriculum as a necessary preliminary to any review' (QCA, 1997:1). This is most welcome. It is a shame upon us all that, at the end of the twentieth century, children in schools in England are following virtually the same curriculum as at the end of the nineteenth. It is also a shame upon us all that maintained schools in this country do not have the resources and facilities to provide the quality and breadth of curriculum that our children need and deserve.

Innumerable books and articles have been written about the school curriculum, its purposes and aims. Many contrasting views and emphases have been expressed. Nevertheless, at the end of the twentieth century there is a widespread view in official, as well as in professional circles, that the 'present statutory arrangements, including the National Curriculum, lack a clear vision of what the parts, individually and collectively, are designed to achieve' (QCA, 1997: 1). Such agreement is hardly surprising. The original aims of the National Curriculum were set out in the most general terms. The Education Reform Act of 1988 stated that a maintained school should have a 'balanced and broadly based curriculum' which

> promotes the spiritual, moral, cultural, mental and physical development of pupils at the school and of society; and prepares such pupils for the opportunities, responsibilities and experiences of adult life.

The precise relationship between these broad aims and the ten subjects of the National Curriculum was never made clear. In 1995 this lack of clarity was further compounded with the formation of the Department for Education and Employment. The aims of education were then redefined without reference to a redefinition of the curriculum itself. The new department declared that:

The Government's principal aim for the education service at all levels and in all forms of learning is:

To support economic growth and improve the nation's competitiveness and quality of life by raising standards of educational achievement and skill and by promoting an efficient and flexible labour market.

(DfEE, 1995: 1)

Since then a new government has come to power, and new educational aims and goals have been set out in the White Paper, *Excellence in Schools*, published in July 1997.

This situation, whereby the aims and objectives of formal education and of the curriculum are regularly and dramatically redrawn by politicians and administrators of central government, without any reference to the school curriculum which they have established, is odd to say the least. It is particularly odd that this should be happening during a five-year moratorium on curriculum change. It suggests that the politicians and administrators of central government believe that radical changes can be made to the aims of education while the curriculum remains the same. It also suggests that the aims of education and of the compulsory school curriculum have become matters of politicking rather than of substance. It is rather like a traveller deciding to go from London to Manchester, while still taking the train to Leeds for which she has a ticket.

In the first contribution to this volume my colleague, John White, has, with his customary incisiveness, tackled the central question: *how should the aims of the revised curriculum be determined?* Two further questions are considered in this section. The first is: *what are the main strengths and weaknesses of common curricula in general and of the National Curriculum in particular?* The second, given that the aims and content of school curricula have been debated for centuries: *what lessons may be drawn from an historical perspective upon these issues?*

Three preliminary points need to be made here to indicate the position from which these questions are to be approached. The first is to reaffirm my frequently stated contention that the application of historical perspectives to human events makes it possible 'to distinguish what is important and long lasting from that which is unimportant and transitory, to identify continuities and changes, and to make judgements as to worth' (Aldrich, 1996: 3). The second point is to concur in the analysis of two further Institute colleagues, Peter Gordon and Denis Lawton, who have maintained that 'curriculum change is the result of complex patterns of interaction between influential individuals and general processes of social, political and economic change' (Gordon and Lawton, 1978: 2). Finally, I endorse the conclusions drawn by John White in his paper as to: the very limited value of making lists of general curriculum aims which have neither internal coherence nor any specific connection with curricular content and delivery; the superiority of liberal democracy over other forms of government (a point I have argued elsewhere, Aldrich, 1997: 13-20); the nature of a democratic political role in the determination of curricular aims and of curricula; the need to avoid sectionalism and to provide for a careful drawing of lines between political and professional spheres of power; the roles of teachers and other educational professionals within democratically determined general aims and broad curricular frameworks; the importance of co-operation between families and schools; the place of knowledge, understanding and dispositions.

The remainder of this paper is arranged in three parts. It begins with a review of the National Curriculum as it exists at present. Strengths and weaknesses, arguments for and against, are identified and discussed. The second part provides one historical perspective by drawing upon the writings of John Locke, the most important educational and political thinker in British history. Finally, conclusions are drawn and answers provided in respect of fundamental curricular aims and curricular provision.

## Strengths and weaknesses

Two broad types of argument in favour of the value and strengths of the National Curriculum may be noted here. The first are those which are adduced in favour of common curricula in general. For example, it is maintained that a common curriculum provides all children with access to that knowledge which is considered to be most worthwhile. It thus avoids the weaknesses apparent in educational systems in which some types of knowledge – including those which are considered to be the most important and prestigious – are reserved to certain groups of children – on social class, gender or other grounds. Differentiated curricula, indeed, may both reflect and reinforce differentiated societies. For example, until well into the second half of the twentieth century, undergraduate student access to the universities of Oxford and Cambridge was restricted to those who could demonstrate their proficiency in the Latin language. No instruction in Latin, however, was provided in most secondary schools. In consequence pupils in such schools were excluded, on curricular grounds, from the two most prestigious seats of higher education in England.

Another argument of this general nature is that a common curriculum furnishes a valuable framework for progression. This has two major benefits. First, it ensures that children do not omit certain topics and repeat others as they move from one year or school to another. Second, a common curriculum may serve as a basis for measuring educational standards and progress – of individual pupils, of schools and teachers, of local educational authorities and of the nation as a whole.

LIVERPOOL JOHN MOORES UNIVERSITY
LEARNING SERVICES

The second, and more specific, type of argument in favour of the National Curriculum of 1988 was the belief that this was an idea whose time had come. Although its introduction and implementation aroused much controversy and opposition, opponents were principally motivated by their loss of control over the curriculum, a control which they had enjoyed for some 40 years. By the 1960s there was considerable support for the idea of a common curriculum based upon a common culture and delivered in common schools. Indeed, by 1975 Denis Lawton was arguing that 'pupils should have access to the same kind of curriculum unless good reasons can be shown for providing different curricula; the onus is on those who wish to provide different curricula, to demonstrate that this will be "fair"' (Lawton, 1975: 116-17). In 1982, Malcolm Skilbeck entitled his inaugural professorial lecture at the Institute of Education, University of London, *A Core Curriculum for the Common School*. Both Lawton and Skilbeck, however, acknowledged the deficiencies of the Schools Council for Curriculum and Examinations, the body established in 1964 to provide for research and development in these two areas. Many curriculum development projects were promoted – some 172 between 1964 and 1978 – but the Schools Council was less effective in providing the type of core curriculum which they both envisaged. Lawton criticized the Schools Council for its 'cafeteria approach' (Lawton, 1978: 13). Skilbeck concluded that while the Schools Council under its revised constitution of 1978 might have been regarded as the best means of establishing a core curriculum, failure to do so led to its justified demise (Skilbeck, 1982:38-9). The National Curriculum of 1988, therefore, may be interpreted as the logical outcome of a movement which commanded widespread professional and political support. Indeed, several initiatives by Labour governments, for example the reorganization of secondary schools under the terms of Circular 10/65, and James Callaghan's Ruskin College speech of 1976 with its emphases upon basic curricula, improved standards and accountability, may be counted as steps on the way towards a common curriculum for a common school. Nevertheless, as Lawton and Skilbeck (among others) acknowledged, little progress was made. It took the very considerable political will and skill of a Conservative

Prime Minister, Margaret Thatcher, and a Conservative Secretary of State for Education, Kenneth Baker, to achieve a common curriculum.

Arguments against the National Curriculum may similarly be divided into two broad groups. The first group are those based not only upon opposition to the National Curriculum of 1988, but also upon opposition to the very principle of a common curriculum. All children, it is argued, are different, and therefore all children need different curricula. Such differences, particularly during the primary school years when all children must acquire the basic skills of reading, writing and arithmetic, may be ones of degree rather than of kind. Nevertheless, it is maintained that curricula should not be based upon the priorities of the producers, but as far as possible upon the needs and choices of the consumers – pupils and their parents. Paradoxically, for many on the political Right the National Curriculum appeared to be an aberration, given that the majority of the clauses of the Education Reform Act of 1988, and the general tenor of Conservative educational and other legislation since 1979, had given such prominence to market forces.

The second type of perceived weakness and attack focused upon the National Curriculum of 1988 itself, and encompassed both content and control. Some critics questioned the idea that the National Curriculum was a natural development. It was argued that the professional insights of teachers, academics and inspectors in the 1970s and 1980s had been jettisoned. The ideal of a common curriculum based upon areas of knowledge and experience, and which drew upon professional expertise and research findings, had been replaced by a backward-looking, subject-based curriculum under political and bureaucratic control (Lawton and Chitty, 1988).

As the following comparison indicates, in reassuming control of the school curriculum, central government appeared to ignore the curriculum development work of some 30 years, reverting instead to a simple list of subjects which almost directly replicated a list produced in the first decade of the twentieth century.

| 1904 Secondary School Regulations | 1988 National Curriculum |
|---|---|
| English | English |
| Mathematics | Mathematics |
| Science | Science |
| History | History |
| Geography | Geography |
| Foreign Language | Foreign Language |
| Drawing | Art |
| Physical Exercise | Physical Education |
| Manual Work/Housewifery | Technology |
|  | Music |

The National Curriculum of 1988 was presented by its proponents and supporters as forward-looking, a curriculum for the twenty-first century. In fact it is largely a traditional curriculum – traditional in its division into subjects and in the very nature of those subjects themselves. It is a National Curriculum which, it has been argued, has been designed to facilitate national testing and to incur minimal expenditure in terms of new types of teachers or facilities.

One further criticism may be noted. While the National Curriculum is compulsory in maintained schools in England (though not in the same form in other parts of the United Kingdom) it does not have to be followed in independent schools. From the beginning it was clear that 'the government believe it would not be right to impose the National Curriculum on independent foundations' (Quoted in Aldrich, 1988: 29). This differentiation between what is required of maintained and of independent schools means that in this sense the National Curriculum of 1988 may be seen not as a common curriculum, but as a divisive one. In the nineteenth century the term, 'National Education', was not used to describe the education of all the children in the nation, but rather of the children of parents who could not, or would not, pay the full costs themselves. The term 'National', in the National Curriculum of 1988, therefore, shows some continuity with this previously divisive, and to some extent demeaning, concept of 'National Education'.

Two points may be made in concluding this section. The first is that common curricula in general and the National Curriculum in particular, have both supporters and opponents, strengths and weaknesses. The second, that it is possible to argue that while the principle of a common curriculum is to be welcomed, the current National Curriculum provides an unsatisfactory example, and is flawed in several respects: its inflexibility even in the face of radical changes in respect of the government's stated aims for education and the linking of education and employment in one ministry; its over-dependence upon subjects; its failure to provide a national base which includes the whole of the United Kingdom and independent as well as maintained schools.

## An historical perspective

John Locke (1632-1704) is the most important political thinker in English history. He was the principal founder of philosophical liberalism, and a champion and codifier of liberal principles in an intolerant age. He is also the most important educational thinker in English history. Locke summed up the educational wisdom and intellectual achievements of previous ages and, through his writings, transformed and transmitted them to future generations. Times, of course, have changed since the seventeenth century, but much of what Locke had to say is timeless. In any discussion about the relationship between a democratic society and the construction of curricular aims and of a school curriculum, John Locke should occupy a central place.

Locke's contemporaries and successors were well aware of his importance and influence. As Samuel Pickering has written:

By 1704, John Yolton argued, 'Locke's epistemological, moral, and religious doctrines' had been so 'thoroughly disseminated both in England and abroad' and had been 'so much discussed, criticized, and praised' that 'no responsible thinker in the eighteenth century could afford to omit reference to Locke.' Of *Some Thoughts*, Richard Aaron wrote simply, 'few other English books have influenced educational thought so deeply.'

(Pickering, 1981: 9)

Locke's importance and influence were widely appreciated and, during the eighteenth century, at least 25 English and 16 French editions of his principal educational work, *Some Thoughts Concerning Education,* were produced, together with others in Dutch, German, Italian and Swedish (Pickering, 1981: 10).

That is not to say that Locke's ideas can simply be translated into the twenty-first century. The social, political and economic conditions of seventeenth-century England were very different from those of today. So too, were some of the educational conditions; for example, compulsory school attendance was not required for a further 200 years, while access to grammar schools and to universities was restricted to males. Nevertheless, certain continuities may also be noted. The universities of Oxford and Cambridge and several grammar schools are still in existence. Some of these schools are now in the independent sector; others in the maintained. Grammar schools were the most distinctive type of school in the medieval and early modern periods. Originally founded in large numbers to teach Latin, the international language of scholarship, law and of the Church, to boys, by the seventeenth century there was less demand for Latin, and many of the new grammar school foundations were making provision for the teaching of English subjects as well (Tompson, 1971: 58). Other establishments, for example charity or parish schools, concentrated upon the basics – which in the seventeenth and eighteenth centuries would have been religion and reading. Most education, of course, still took place outside of school, and was social, religious and vocational both in content and in context.

Some of the religious dimensions of formal education have lasted until today, but over the last two centuries the growing predominance of secular over religious educational aims has been apparent. In Locke's day, as throughout the 300 years following the Reformation of the 1530s, although formal educational institutions were largely local in character, ultimate control of education was in the hands of the state and of the state Church. Religious and social aims predominated in curricular matters. In August 1840, instructions issued by James Phillips Kay (later Kay-Shuttleworth) on behalf of the Committee of the Privy Council, the new central authority for education, to the first two members of Her Majesty's Inspectorate of Schools, John Allen and Hugh Seymour Tremenheere, advised that:

> Their Lordships are strongly of opinion that no plan of education ought to be encouraged in which the intellectual instruction is not subordinate to the regulation of the thoughts and habits of the children by the doctrines and precepts of revealed religion.
>
> (Minutes of the Committee of Council on Education, 1840-1: 3)

Some 20 years later, however, the Revised Code of 1862 marked an important change in emphasis. Although inspectors were still required to examine children in religious knowledge, the system of payment by results introduced in that year was based upon the performance of pupils in the three secular subjects of reading, writing and arithmetic. The growth of secular, as opposed to religious, aims in curriculum matters is but one of the fundamental changes that can be observed across the centuries. Others include the incorporation of science into the curriculum, a process furthered by the National Curriculum of 1988 which extended the grammar school curriculum of 1904 to all secondary and primary schools. Even more fundamental changes have seen a reduction in the differentiation in curricular aims and provision which existed in the seventeenth century – a differentiation based on social hierarchies and gender. Until the beginning of the twentieth century much of the education of the children of the poor was aimed at teaching them to recognize their betters (which in the case of girls included their husbands) and to defer to them.

But though there have been changes in curricular aims and in curricula, there have also been continuities. The personal, social and moral education of children, construed and constructed across the centuries within a religious framework, remains a central concern. The promotion of civil peace and social cohesion through education is as important in the twenty-first century as it was in Tudor and Stuart times. The issue of securing an appropriate balance between moral, academic and vocational education has been a constant, as has the place of formal schooling within education in general. There is no space here to consider all of the curriculum continuities and changes which connect and divide the seventeenth and twenty-first centuries. They have been treated in a recent work (Aldrich, 1996: 23-39) which also provides historical perspectives upon the accompanying themes of access, standards and assessment, teaching quality, control, economic performance and consumers. But it is important to note that key tensions about curricular aims, content, context and delivery – child centred or subject based, academic or vocational, religious or secular, moral or knowledge-centred, common or diverse – are nothing new. They have long histories.

John Locke's claim to be the most important educationist in English history depends upon three factors. The first is that he was himself an educator, both of children and of adults. The second, that Locke's range of interests and qualities traversed a number of fields. Indeed, he made important contributions to knowledge, not only in education but also in political philosophy, science, medicine, psychology, economics and theology. The third is that in each of these fields Locke acts as a hinge between the medieval and modern worlds. As Peter Gay has concluded, 'John Locke was the father of the Enlightenment in educational thought as in much else...His treatise on education stands at the beginning of the long cycle of modernity, but it stands, too, at the end, and as the climax, of a long evolution – the discovery of the child' (Gay, 1964: 1).

There is no space in this paper to provide a substantial account of Locke's political philosophy. His place in British history is bound up with the concept of the 'Glorious Revolution' of 1688, but he is equally admired in the United States. As Tarcov has claimed:

> there is a very real sense in which Americans can say that Locke is *our* political philosopher. The document by virtue of which we Americans are an independent people ... derives its principles and even some of its language from the political philosophy of John Locke.
>
> (Tarcov, 1984: 1)

Similarly, only a brief summary of his life is possible here. Born in 1632 at Wrington in Somerset, Locke's father was an attorney and small landowner who served as a captain in the Parliamentary army during the Civil War against King Charles I. In 1647, at the age of 15, Locke was sent to Westminster School in London, then under the direction of the famous headmaster, Dr Richard Busby, a scholar, a firm believer in flogging, and a supporter of the Royalist cause. In 1652 Locke gained a scholarship to Christ Church, Oxford. There he was attracted by elements of the new learning, and followed a wide curriculum – the traditional studies of classics, rhetoric, logic, morals and geometry, together with mathematics, astronomy, history, Hebrew, Arabic, natural philosophy, botany, chemistry and medicine. In 1660 he was appointed to a lectureship in Greek, and held a number of College offices before taking up a post in 1667 as tutor and physician in the household of Anthony Ashley Cooper, Baron Ashley. At Exeter House in the Strand, Shaftesbury's London home, Locke fulfilled a variety of roles. He acted as tutor and medical adviser to Shaftesbury's sickly young heir, and subsequently arranged his marriage to Lady Dorothy Manners. He attended Lady Dorothy during her several deliveries and miscarriages and oversaw the education of her seven children. In 1672, his employer was created first Earl of Shaftesbury and Lord Chancellor. Locke thus gained some entry to the political world, and indeed held minor public office as Secretary of Presentations of Benefices and Secretary of the Council of Trade and Plantations. Between 1675 and 1679 Locke was in France, where he travelled and read widely, and spent some months acting as tutor to Caleb, the son of Sir John Banks. Following Shaftesbury's disgrace, and death in Holland in January 1683, Locke also took up residence in Holland, where he lived until 1689. The last years of his life were spent as a paying guest in the house of Sir Francis and Lady Masham at Oates in Essex.

Locke lived in the most turbulent age in modern English history. He was a boy during the Civil War, and a pupil at Westminster when, on 30 January 1649, King Charles I was executed at Whitehall, just a short distance from the school. His employer, Shaftesbury, was twice imprisoned in the Tower of London, and forced to flee for his life. Locke was stripped of his government posts, and came under considerable suspicion as a traitor, not least in Royalist Oxford. Even in Holland, Locke thought it prudent to adopt an assumed name and to keep on the move. A cautious, careful man, not until February 1689, following the proclamation by Parliament of William and Mary as king and queen, did Locke deem it safe to return to England. His new-found political favour was demonstrated by William's offers of the post of ambassador to the Elector of Brandenburg (which Locke declined) and the post of Commissioner of Appeals. For Locke, however, the most important outcome of life under the new regime was that he now deemed it possible to publish his major works: the *Letters Concerning Toleration* (1689, 1690, 1692 and posthumous fragment), *An Essay Concerning Human Understanding* (1690), *Two Treatises of Government* (1690), the *Reasonableness of Christianity* (1695), and the work upon which his reputation as an educator mainly rests, *Some Thoughts Concerning Education* (1693).

This very brief account of Locke and his times indicates his range of experiences – educational, political, commercial, medical, scientific, religious and philosophical. His educational ideas were the products of these experiences, and his approach to the aims and content of the curriculum was broad and balanced. This breadth of experience must have been complemented on the many occasions on which he feared for his freedom, and indeed for his life, by a depth of understanding of those values and knowledge which should be counted as being of greatest worth.

*Some Thoughts Concerning Education*, though first published in 1693, was based upon a series of letters which Locke wrote between 1684 and 1687 from Holland to a friend and distant relative, Edward Clarke, who had asked about the education of his son. The *Thoughts*, therefore, are not a systematic treatise on education, but are based upon a considered response to a specific situation and request. They were not intended as a blueprint for the schooling of all children. Locke's advice was aimed principally at parents and tutors. He certainly did not believe that in his own day the education suitable for the son of a gentleman could be universally applied. Nevertheless, fundamental elements of universality do occur in Locke's writings. The *Essay Concerning Human Understanding* was a general inquiry into the origins, certainties and extent of human knowledge, and the first French translation of the *Thoughts* appeared in 1695 under the title *De l'éducation des Enfans*. Indeed, in his preface to this edition Pierre Coste stated that although Locke's work was particularly designed for the education of gentlemen,

> This does not prevent its serving also for the education of all sorts of children, of whatever class they are: for if you except that which the author says about exercises that a young gentleman ought to learn, nearly all the rules that he gives, are universal.
>
> (Quoted in Axtell, 1968: 52)

Although the historical circumstances in which Locke lived and wrote must be borne in mind, there is no doubt that his thoughts about the importance, purpose, methods and content of education have considerable relevance for the twenty-first century. Education was his priority, and Locke's belief in the importance of education is demonstrated by his statement in the first paragraph of the *Thoughts* that 'of all the men we meet with, nine parts of ten are what they are, good or evil, useful or not, by their education'. For Locke, the purpose of education was to produce virtuous and healthy human beings. As far as possible, teaching was to be by example rather than by rules, by the formation of good habits, and by a humane approach characterized by rationality rather than by corporal punishment. The

I.M. MARSH LIBRARY LIVERPOOL L17 6BD
TEL. 0151 231 5216/5299

curriculum, though broad, should be adapted to the child's interests and abilities. Such principles are universal and may be universally applied.

The *Thoughts* began with a quotation from Juvenal (c.55-c.140), the Roman lawyer and satirist, that 'A sound mind in a sound body is a short, but full description of a happy state in this world'. *Mens sana in corpore sano*, indeed, is a valuable statement of the aims of education and of life in general, both for children and for adults, and as applicable in the year 2000 and beyond as in the first, second or seventeenth centuries. As a doctor, Locke placed considerable emphasis upon the physical well-being of children. Indeed, the first section of the *Thoughts* deals with child health and contains much good advice on 'plenty of open air, exercise and sleep, plain diet, no wine or strong drink, and very little or no physick' (*Thoughts*, section 30). The relevance of this advice is immediately apparent. The current National Curriculum does not give sufficient attention to physical well-being. Many state schools and colleges are forced to provide education in outmoded, inadequate and dilapidated buildings. Few have adequate exercise facilities and playing fields. Some, indeed, have been forced by financial constraints to dispose of land rather than to acquire it. One of the most obvious discrepancies between the facilities and curricula of independent and maintained schools is to be found in their respective provisions for physical exercise. For some children, it is only through holiday camps conducted at independent schools that they are able to enjoy the exercise and sports facilities which should be theirs by right under a proper national curriculum. For the majority of children, however, such access is permanently denied. Locke's concern about diet is also pertinent for our times. While this might not be thought to be a curriculum matter, it is a shame that public concern for the diet of children, once demonstrated in the provision of school meals and milk, has been allowed to lapse. Such provision was introduced at the beginning of the twentieth century because it was recognized that the capacities of some children to learn were being seriously inhibited by poor nutrition. At the end of the century, poverty and ignorance ensure that many children in this country still suffer from an inadequate diet.

Locke's views on a sound mind embraced many dimensions. He did not advocate cramming the mind full of indigestible and unintelligible information, but emphasized rather the importance of the formation of good habits from an early age, of paying attention to the child's real needs, of using esteem and disgrace rather than corporal punishment in the disciplining of children, and of the need for good parental example. These precepts are of a methodological or pedagogical nature, but Locke's hierarchy of values – virtue, wisdom, breeding and learning – designed originally for the son of a gentleman, provides important perspectives upon the knowledge-based society and its subject-based National Curriculum.

For Locke, one of the most knowledgeable men of his day, virtue was the true end of education. Almost half of the sections in the *Thoughts* are concerned with this aim. Virtue was to be promoted by simple acts of religious observance and faith, by the denying of selfish desires and by a concern for credit and good reputation. For a gentleman, virtue was 'absolutely requisite to make him valued and beloved by others, acceptable or tolerable to himself' (*Thoughts*, section 135). This did not mean any holier-than-thou attitude. Locke's concern for virtue as the chief end of education was of a practical kind, and expressed in his support for certain virtues. These have been well summarized by Tarcov who has written that 'The Lockean virtues are self-denial, civility, liberality, justice, courage, humanity, curiosity (or, more properly, industry), and truthfulness' (Tarcov, 1984: 189).

Wisdom, for Locke, was similarly of a practical kind – managing one's time, money and resources to the best advantage, with openness and sincerity. He made a sharp distinction between cunning and wisdom. Wisdom was an essential quality for securing a good reputation, whereas 'a cunning trick helps but once, but hinders ever after' (*Thoughts*, section 140). Wisdom, which can only be fully developed in adulthood, is hard to come by, involving as it does the acquisition of a true knowledge of the world and of the individuals in it.

Good breeding meant treading a middle way between 'sheepish bashfulness' on the one hand, and a bullying, hectoring, disrespectful manner on the other. Locke's aim was the cultivation of civility, which he identified as 'this first, and most taking of all the social virtues' (*Thoughts*, section 143). His golden rule for achieving this virtue was 'not to think meanly of ourselves, and not to think meanly of others' (*Thoughts*, section 141). Children, however, could not be taught civility by rules alone. Shamefacedness and confusion in thoughts, words and looks could only be overcome by encouraging children to behave in all company, whether in the home or outside, 'with that freedom and gracefulness, which pleases, and makes them acceptable' (*Thoughts*, section 142). Locke's emphasis upon the importance of reasoned discussion and respect for the views of opponents is particularly apposite today when so many areas of life – including politics and the media – are characterized by confrontation. He abhorred 'frequent interruptions in arguing, and loud wrangling' and noted that:

> The Indians, whom we call barbarous, observe much more decency and civility in their discourses and conversation, giving one another a fair silent hearing, till they have quite done; and then answering them calmly and without noise or passion. And if it be not so in this civilized part of the world, we must impute it to a neglect in education, which has not yet reformed this ancient piece of barbarity amongst us.
>
> (*Thoughts*, section 145)

Finally, Locke came to learning. He acknowledged that his readers might

> wonder, perhaps that I put learning last, especially if I tell you that I think it the least part. This may be seem strange in the mouth of a bookish man...this being almost that alone, which is thought on, when people talk of education, makes it the greater paradox.
>
> (*Thoughts*, section 157)

How is that paradox to be explained? In relegating learning to the last place in curricular aims, Locke sought to reverse the widespread assumption that education consisted mainly of teaching children large amounts of factual academic knowledge. He particularly wanted to draw attention to the excessive concentration upon Latin and Greek in the grammar schools of his day and to the excessive punishments employed to instill such learning into children. Locke wanted all children to learn the basics – to read, to be able to express themselves clearly both orally and on paper, and to count – but he was opposed to the unexamined domination of the curriculum by traditional subjects.

As Locke well knew, in his own day (as in ours) the very scope and nature of knowledge was being transformed. Yet in Locke's day, as in ours, the acquisition of certain types of academic knowledge predominated in many schools, to the detriment both of other types of academic knowledge, and of moral, personal, social, aesthetic, physical, practical and vocational education. Schools were dominated by a narrow, subject-based curriculum which reflected custom and tradition. This situation had arisen as a result of a failure to consider the true aims of education and to apply them to the curriculum. 'How else is it possible' Locke asked, 'that a child should be chained to the oar, seven, eight or ten of the best years of his life, to get a language or two?' (*Thoughts*, section 147).

Locke's advice on curriculum was sound and balanced: reading should be taught at the earliest possible age, with picture books rather than sacred scriptures as texts; drawing and writing, including shorthand for the purpose of making quick notes; French and Latin by the conversational method; arithmetic, geometry, accounts, geography and history; science; accomplishments; and at least one (and preferably two or three) manual trades, even for the sons of gentlemen. Locke, who was himself a keen gardener, saw several purposes in manual training: the promotion of physical well-being, relief from too much bookish learning, the ability to earn a living.

# Conclusions

Six conclusions may be drawn.

The first is that since the introduction of the National Curriculum in 1988 the relationship between the aims of education as expressed by central government and the school curriculum has been unclear. Indeed, there would appear to have been virtually no connection at all. The decision of QCA to begin the process of review by focusing upon aims, rather than upon a list of subjects, is most welcome. The current list of subjects is no starting point for the creation of a national curriculum for the twenty-first century. Not only should the list of aims precede the list of subjects, the very concept of a curriculum which is essentially presented as a list of subjects should be called into question. Connections between curricular aims, location, content and delivery must be made clear. They must also be respected. There should be no future restatements of aims and purposes without acknowledgment of the effects of such restatements upon the location, content and delivery of the curriculum.

One effect of beginning the process of curricular revision with aims rather than with subjects is to emphasize the need for such aims to be broadly understood (and to the greatest possible extent shared) by all those concerned with education – pupils, parents, teachers, administrators, politicians, employers. A truly national curriculum will involve all of these groups not only at the level of planning, but also of delivery. A national curriculum should not simply be confined to the education provided in schools, but should be framed with reference to education throughout the community, in the family and home, in the club and church, and in the workplace. It is clear that a genuine reform of the existing National Curriculum will not simply require changes to the current list of subjects. It will also necessitate a reconsideration of the relationship between school subjects and areas of knowledge and experience, a change in the relationship between schools and education, a strengthening of the family and workplace as educational environments, and a modification or supplementation of the role of classroom teacher by means of the family or group tutor. A new partnership is required, one which will include the media, and be based upon mutual recognition of roles and responsibilities. The practical problems associated with such fundamental reform may be considerable. There are bound to be costs, not least in respect of teachers, facilities and equipment. There will also be wider costs, consequent upon an appreciation of the educational importance of the environments in which children are brought up. But the first and the most substantial task is to replace the confrontational and proprietary culture that has built up around education and which so soured the introduction of the National Curriculum of 1988.

The third conclusion is to note that in recent years, principally as a result of central government interventions, the historical (and philosophical) dimensions of educational study have been virtually eliminated from the education and training of prospective and practising teachers, and from discussions of educational planning and policy making. At this historic moment in time, when a revised national curriculum is to be put in place for the twenty-first century, it is essential to recognize that such questions as 'What are the aims of education?' or 'What knowledge is of most worth?' have long histories. John Locke is but one of those who have considered such questions and whose answers provide important perspectives upon our current discussions. It is to be hoped that the current revision of curricular aims will make full use of historical perspectives. Such perspectives make it possible to explore both the nature and processes of continuities and changes and to identify those elements which are of permanent and greatest worth. In a piece of this length it has only been possible to provide an introduction to such perspectives and to furnish the briefest of summaries of the life and educational thought of one individual who died some 300 years ago. A much fuller picture, and more substantial analysis could be provided by considering perspectives drawn from the work of other prominent thinkers about the curriculum. These might include such diverse and more modern figures as J.H. Badley, the founder of Bedales School, and Lawrence Stenhouse, director of the Humanities Curriculum

Project funded by the Nuffield Foundation and the Schools Council and founder of the Centre for Applied Research in Education at the University of East Anglia (Aldrich and Gordon, 1989: 14-15, 237-8), Nevertheless, as Peter Gay has rightly concluded, although the society, and therefore the educational structures of Locke's day were very different from our own, and though many of Locke's specific recommendations may seem to be irrelevant or out of date, the roots of what is valuable in modern educational philosophy are to be found in *Some Thoughts Concerning Education.*

> And more: if we want to remind ourselves why we really wish to educate children, if we seek a philosophy that insists on the relevance of subject matter to experience without neglecting the pleasure of cultivation for its own sake, that emphasizes recognition of the child's needs without ignoring the uses of discipline, that urges the relation of morale to learning without denying the virtue of hard study, that seeks to form men and women fit for modern life without forgetting that this fitness requires cultivation of the higher sensibilities and a profound knowledge of the great literature of the past – if we seek such an educational theory we would do well to read, and reread, Locke with care.
>
> (Gay, 1964: 15)

Since the seventeenth century, the amount of learning in the world has greatly increased – particularly in such areas as science and technology. Today, these subjects occupy a pride of place similar to that once enjoyed by religion and the classical languages. In the twenty-first century this process of change is bound to continue, and most children and adults will need a greater and/or different range of knowledge and of skills in order to participate successfully in society. This will require the creation of a national curriculum that is both more responsive to change, and better tailored to the aptitudes and abilities of individual pupils. A significant modification of the prescription of subjects and of specific programmes of study is needed. Not that everything will change; many of the traditional elements in knowledge and learning – for example, reading, writing and mathematics – will retain their importance.

Though much of the knowledge and many of the skills required in the twenty-first century may change, the nature and primacy of values will remain constant. Locke's emphasis upon the importance of virtue, wisdom and civility is enduring; his advice that 'Learning must be had, but in the second place, as subservient only to greater qualities' (*Thoughts*, section 147) provides a timely corrective to narrow, subject-based curricula in any age. The values that Locke espoused – self-denial, civility, liberality, justice, courage, humanity, industry and truthfulness – are universal. Such qualities are essential not only for the well-being of the individual, but also for the well-being of society and of the state. In the long run it profits none of us if individuals, groups or nations gain considerable knowledge and power and yet lack the qualities necessary to exercise such knowledge and power for the general good.

Finally, it is important to note that some actions must be taken immediately, not only to prepare for an improved national curriculum but also to protect that currently in existence. In June 1997 the Labour government announced that future sales of playing fields would be blocked. Nevertheless, in December 1997 a report by the National Playing Fields Association revealed that 5,000 school pitches had been sold since 1981, and that some five pitches per week were still being lost (*Sunday Times*, 28 December 1997).

## Note

I am grateful to William J. Reese, Deborah Spring and John White for comments on earlier versions of this paper. The quotations from the *Thoughts* have been rendered into modern form and are taken from James L. Axtell's 1968 edition of Locke's educational writings.

# REFERENCES

Aldrich, R. (1988), 'The National Curriculum: an Historical Perspective'. In D. Lawton and C. Chitty (eds), *The National Curriculum*. London: Institute of Education.

— (1996), *Education for the Nation*. London: Institute of Education.

— (1997), *The End of History and the Beginning of Education*. London: Institute of Education.

Aldrich, R. and Gordon, P. (1989), *Dictionary of British Educationists*. London: Woburn.

Antidote (1997), *The Antidote* No.2. October 1997.

Axtell, J.L. (ed.) (1968), *The Educational Writings of John Locke*. Cambridge: Cambridge University Press.

Department for Education and Employment (1995), *The English Education System: an Overview of Structure and Policy*. London: DfEE.

Gay, P. (ed.) (1964), *John Locke on Education*. New York: Teachers College.

Goleman, D. (1996), *Emotional Intelligence*. London: Bloomsbury.

Gordon, P. and Lawton, D. (1978), *Curriculum Change in the Nineteenth and Twentieth Centuries*. London: Hodder & Stoughton.

Gray, J. (1995), *Berlin*. London: Fontana.

Hamlyn, D.W. (1967), 'Logical and psychological aspects of learning'. In R.S. Peters (ed.) *The Concept of Education*. London: Routledge & Kegan Paul.

Harrison, R. (1993), *Democracy*. London: Routledge.

Hirst, P.H. (1974), 'Liberal Education and the nature of Knowledge' reprinted in his *Knowledge and the Curriculum*. London: Routledge & Kegan Paul.

Lawton, D. (1975), *Class, Culture and the Curriculum*. London: Routledge & Kegan Paul.

— (1978), *The End of the Secret Garden? A Study in the Politics of the Curriculum*. London: Institute of Education.

Lawton, D. and Chitty, C. (eds) (1988), *The National Curriculum*. London: Institute of Education.

Miller, D. (1995), *On Nationality*. Oxford: Oxford University Press.

O'Hear, P. and White, J. (1991), *A National Curriculum for All: Laying the Foundations for Success*. London: IPPR.

Peters, R.S. (1996), *Ethics and Education*. London: Allen & Unwin.

Pickering, S.F. (1981), *John Locke and Children's Books in Eighteenth-Century England*. Knoxville: University of Tennessee Press.

Qualifications and Curriculum Council (1997), *Aims for the School Curriculum 5-16*. London: QCA.

SCAA (1996), *Consultation on values in education and in the community*.

Skilbeck, M. (1982), *A Core Curriculum for the Common School*. London: Institute of Education.

Talbot, M. and Tate, N. (1997), 'Shared values in a pluralist society?'. In R. Smith and P. Standish (eds.) *Teaching Right and Wrong: moral education in the balance*. Stoke-on-Trent: Trentham.

Tarcov, N. (1984), *Locke's Education for Liberty*. Chicago: University of Chicago Press.

Tompson, R.S. (1971), *Classics or Charity? The Dilemma of the Eighteenth-Century Grammar School*. Manchester University Press.

White, J. (1975), 'The end of the compulsory curriculum' in *The Curriculum: The Doris Lee Lectures* . London: Institute of Education.

— (1990), *Education and the Good Life: beyond the National Curriculum*. London: Kogan Page.

— (1998), *Do Howard Gardner's multiple intelligences add up?* London: Institute of Education.